わたしの ヒロシマ

Junko Morimoto

MY HIROSHIMA

Junko Morimoto

Hiroshima is the town of my memories. It is surrounded
by green mountains and looks towards the sea. Through
it flow seven beautiful rivers.

VIKING

I was the smallest in our family. There was my father and mother, my brother and two elder sisters.

Sometimes I liked to be alone. I would stay at home and draw many things — all day I would draw, it was what I loved most.

I had many friends but my best friends were Fumi and
Haruko. We played lots of games — our favourite was
"Oranges and Lemons".

Summertime was fireworks time.
It was fun going with my family to
watch the beautiful colours and
patterns as they burst overhead.
They looked so large and high
above the bridge where we stood.

I didn't like going to school. Every morning I would hold tightly to my brother's jacket and follow behind him.

My teacher wore glasses with heavy, black frames. I liked
him best when he taught us painting.

In the winter of my fourth year at school, a big war
started.

As I grew up, the world around me changed a lot. By the time I reached high school I had to wear special clothes, because the war our country was in influenced everything.

There were fewer and fewer goods in the shops.
Everyone had to spend their summer holidays doing
military exercises.

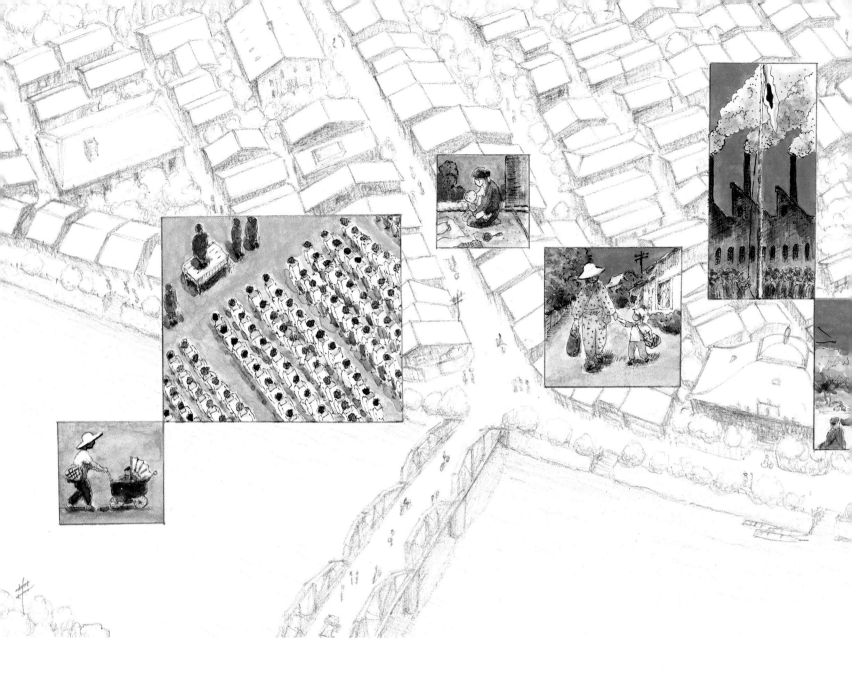

8.15 AM   AUGUST 6   1945

The people of Hiroshima had just begun their day's work. Suddenly, the sirens sounded, warning that a plane was approaching, but the sirens soon stopped and everyone went about their work.

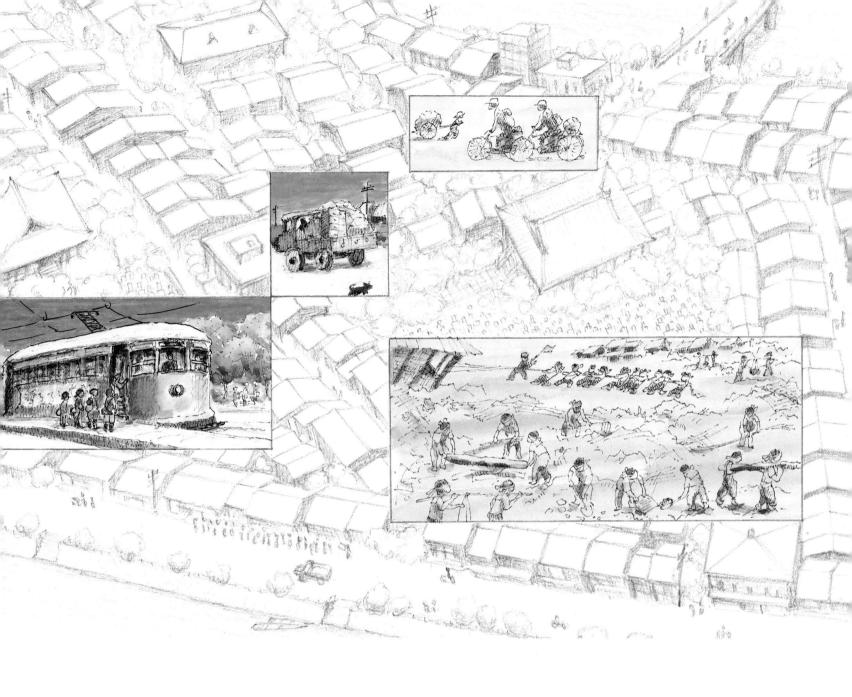

This day I had a pain in my stomach and was not going to school. My sister and I were in our room talking.

I thought I heard the sound of a plane, but it seemed a
long way off and very high up.

I was hit by a thunderous flash and
an explosion of sound.

My eyes burnt — everything went
black. I held my sister.

Everything faded away — I thought I
was dying.

I woke up. I was alive. But my home was completely destroyed.

When I crawled outside, I found that the whole of Hiroshima was destroyed. Everything was blown away, torn apart. Everything was burning.

The banks of the river were crowded with people,
everyone wanted to be near the water.

There was a child, screaming, trying to wake-up her
dead mother.

I was very lucky, my family were all alive and we were together, sheltering in a cave.

Father's face was badly burnt and swollen. My brother's back was full of pieces of glass from the window he was sitting beneath. My eldest sister had her teeth sticking through her lip, she had been using chopsticks.

We watched as hundreds and hundreds of people escaped from burning Hiroshima, under the strong sunlight of summer.

Every school became a hospital for the badly injured.
I heard people screaming and moaning in pain, and
there was a horrible smell of burnt skin.

Many people died, one after another. Their bodies were
taken to the school's playing field and burnt.

Several days later we heard the announcement
that the war was over.

Half a year passed.

The students who had survived went back to their schools. From the dirt of the burnt earth I took an aluminium lunch box with burnt, black rice inside. I found the bones of many of my friends.

Many, many years have passed and I have returned to my
school again.

It is still a miracle that I survived.

All I see now is clean white ground and peaceful images
of young students, who are just like I was so long ago.

THE FACTS ABOUT HIROSHIMA

At 8.15 a.m. on August 6, 1945, an atomic bomb was dropped on the Japanese city of Hiroshima. This was the first time such a bomb had been used in warfare:

- 70,000 people died instantly

- another 70,000 died by the end of 1945

- at the end of 1950 the total was 200,000

- even today people are dying who survived the initial blast.

These figures are estimates, supplied by the city of Hiroshima in a report for the United Nations.

This report also states that within 1.5 kilometres of the hypocentre, the bomb blast would have been the equivalent of a hurricane with a wind force of 90 metres per second.

Every year on the 6 August, the city of Hiroshima hosts a remembrance ceremony which thousands of people from around the world attend.

ACKNOWLEDGEMENTS

EDITOR: ANNE BOWER INGRAM
DESIGNERS: JUNKO MORIMOTO AND TREVOR HOOD
TEXT: Written in Japanese by Junko Morimoto
Translated and adapted into English by ISAO MORIMOTO AND ANNE BOWER INGRAM
PHOTOGRAPHS: All historical photographs kindly reproduced with the permission of the Hiroshima newspaper the CHŪGOKU SHINBUN
Photograph of modern Hiroshima by MASAYUKI YOSHIDA
Photograph of Junko Morimoto by ISAO MORIMOTO

VIKING

Published by the Penguin Group
Viking Penguin, a division of Penguin Books USA Inc.,
375 Hudson Street New York, New York 10014, U.S.A.
Penguin Books Ltd, 27 Wrights Lane, London W8 5TZ, England
Penguin Books Australia Ltd, Ringwood, Victoria, Australia
Penguin Books Canada Ltd, 10 Alcorn Avenue, Toronto, Ontario, Canada M4V 3B2
Penguin Books (N.Z.) Ltd, 182–190 Wairau Road, Auckland 10, New Zealand

Penguin Books Ltd, Registered Offices: Harmondsworth, Middlesex, England

First published in Australia by William Collins Pty Ltd, 1987

First American edition published in 1990

3 5 7 9 10 8 6 4 2

Copyright © Junko Morimoto, 1987

All rights reserved

Library of Congress Catalog Card Number: 89-51483
ISBN: 0-670-83181-6

Printed in China

LET ALL THE SOULS HERE REST IN PEACE,
FOR WE SHALL NOT REPEAT THE EVIL.